DIARY OF A TIME TRAVELER

NICHOLAS STEVENSON

DAVID LONG

1 MILLION BC-1969
DIARY CONTENTS

VOTES FOR WOMEN

PAGES 6-7
1 MILLION BC, AFRICA
LIGHTING THE FIRST FIRE

PAGES 8-9
2000 BC, BRITAIN
BUILDING STONEHENGE

PAGES 42-43
1805, USA
CROSSING AMERICA WITH LEWIS AND CLARK

PAGES 10-11
1332 BC, EGYPT
MEETING THE BOY PHARAOH

PAGES 40-41
1761, AUSTRIA
MAKING MUSIC WITH MOZART

PAGES 44-45
1843, BRITAIN
CHECKING OUT THE FIRST COMPUTER

PAGES 12-13
448 BC, GREECE
WATCHING THE EARLY OLYMPICS

PAGES 46-47
1865, USA
CHEERING AN END TO SLAVERY

PAGES 60-61
1969, THE MOON
MANKIND'S GIANT LEAP...

PAGES 14-15
211 BC, CHINA
WALKING THE GREAT WALL

PAGES 18-19
AD 970, CHINA
FIREWORKS FIT FOR A KING

PAGES 22-23
1200, MEXICO
SPOTTING THE SUN SERPENT

PAGES 48-49
1899, RUSSIA
CROSSING A FROZEN LAKE

PAGES 16-17
AD 80, ITALY
GETTING READY FOR THE GLADIATORS

PAGES 20-21
AD 1000, CANADA
SAILING TO THE NEW WORLD

It all started when I fell asleep in history class. Next thing I knew, there was a sharp knocking on my desk, and Professor Tempo was standing over me looking distinctly unimpressed.

"Keeping you up, are we, Augustus?" she asked, one eyebrow raised. I sighed. "Sorry, but history is just a bit... you know. Boring."

"Boring?" Now she looked even more unimpressed. "I'll tell you what— I'll show you something to change your mind."

She gave me this book, full of blank pages, and a little yellow pencil. "Why do you think the world is as it is today?" she asked.

"Don't you ever wonder who invented all the incredible things around us? Where our buildings, languages, customs, and technologies come from? Imagine if you could go back in time a million years! Wouldn't you like to see for yourself how the world has changed since then?"

"Yeah, like that's going to happen!" I scoffed.

"Go home tonight," she said, "and think about an event from history that you'd like to find out more about. Write it on the first page of this book, then get ready."

"For what?"

"Just wait," replied the professor, heading for the door. As she left, she looked over her shoulder and winked. "See you later," she said.

Once humans had learned to **COOK**, they could eat new sorts of plants and animals.

WHOAAAAAAAA!

Fire meant that people could be active at **NIGHT** as well as during the day.

PREHISTORIC PEOPLE used fire to make clay pots and simple stone or metal weapons.

By melting sand over fire, people were able to make **COLORED GLASS**—one of the earliest types of jewelry.

Whoa! What a ride! So suddenly I found myself in a cave a MILLION YEARS AGO! Who would have thought it? The professor was there, too, which was good because otherwise I would have been a bit freaked out.

Now, the people in these parts were our ancient ancestors, and the prof told me they were called "*Homo erectus*." Their cave was pretty basic, but I guess that was to be expected, and at least it gave them some shelter from the weather and the wild animals prowling around outside. Anyway, it turned out we got there just in time to witness them making humankind's first-ever fire. I know—awesome, eh?

From what I could see in the gloom, the bright flames scared them at first, but gradually they moved closer, huddling together to enjoy the warmth and light. Professor Tempo said that soon they'd learn to use the fire to defend themselves against the wild animals, and then they'd get to grips with cooking meat. Shame they couldn't cook anything yet—I could have gone for a burger...

DRUIDS, or PRIESTS, may have been in charge of the design of Stonehenge.

Some of the stones were transported over **155 MILES** from Wales!

The prof said that because there are 28 pages left in this diary, we could only visit 28 more places, so I needed to think carefully about where to go next.

Stonehenge was one of the oldest man-made constructions I could think of, so I decided to see how they built it without backhoes or cranes.

The place was a hive of activity. The first thing I noticed was the number of people—hundreds of them. Some were cutting gigantic stones into shape, while others struggled to move them around.

Some of the stones were totally enormous and apparently weighed as much as ten elephants. The workers used leather ropes and rollers made of tree trunks to transport them—I counted almost 500 men moving just one massive stone! Seems that building the world's most famous prehistoric monument was no easy feat.

We don't know why Stonehenge was built, but it could have been a temple, a strange kind of calendar, or a place of healing, according to the prof. Even with all these people working away, it took decades to complete. They'd be pleased to know that it's still standing 4,000 years later!

1332 BC, EGYPT
MEETING THE BOY PHARAOH

Egypt's military chief, **HOREMHAB**, was another of Tutankhamen's important advisers.

AY was one of the young king's closest advisers. He later became pharaoh himself.

The pharaoh's teacher, **SENNEDJEM**, was an important figure in his life but fell out of favor after Tutankhamen came to the throne.

TUTANKHAMEN wore sandals with pictures of his enemies on the soles so wherever he walked he trampled them underfoot!

Next up, I thought it would be cool to take a trip to ancient Egypt 3,000 years ago. As luck would have it, we arrived in the middle of a coronation.

I asked the professor who was being made king, and she pointed to a boy who looked about my age. Crazy, huh? Just imagine being pharaoh and everyone having to do what you say!

The young pharaoh's name was Tutankhamen and the ceremony was pretty amazing. There were loads of guys in masks (priests, apparently) and everyone was dressed in really fancy robes.

One of the priests gave Tutankhamen a crook and flail—the professor says they were signs of kingship back then, like a crown today. Then he was led off to be dunked in a sacred pool before coming back to sit on a golden throne. He looked a bit scared, but I suppose that's not surprising. The prof told me that his reign was really short—he died at age 19, only ten years later, which I thought was sad.

QUEEN NEFERTITI was married to Tutankhamen's father, Akhenaten. She was a powerful figure and may have ruled the kingdom briefly after her husband's death.

In ancient Egypt, kings were thought to be gods. To keep the bloodline pure, TUTANKHAMEN'S MOTHER may also have been his father's sister.

Tutankhamen's beloved nurse, MAIA, remained close to him throughout his short life.

DORIEÚS was the youngest son of Diagoras of Rhodes. He was too young to compete at these games, but grew up to be a champion.

I LOVE sports, so I wanted to get a track-side view at the Olympics... 2,500 years ago!

The first-ever Olympics were in 776 BC, but there was only one race, so I was happy to be there a bit later, with more events to watch.

These ancient Olympics were not quite what I'd expected. Firstly, the competitors had no clothes on! I was a bit shocked, but the professor reassured me that in ancient Greece people always exercised naked (in fact, the word "gymnasium" comes from the Greek word "gymnós," which means "naked").

The other thing I noticed was that there were no women competitors, and apparently married women weren't even allowed to watch, on pain of death—pretty harsh, eh? Instead of medals, the winners were given crowns of olive leaves and were paraded around on people's shoulders.

The most impressive thing was an incredible temple with this enormous—truly massive—statue of the king of the Greek gods, Zeus. It was taller than a five-story building, all covered in gold. The professor tells me that it was one of the Seven Wonders of the Ancient World, but was destroyed in a fire about 1,500 years ago. What a feeling to have seen it in the flesh!

211 BC, CHINA
WALKING THE GREAT WALL

When the Great Wall of China was completed, it had a total length of over **13,000 MILES**!

ANQI SHENG was a legendary wizard believed to be 1,000 years old. The emperor wanted to find out the secret of long life from him.

An army of more than 8,000 **TERRA-COTTA SOLDIERS** was buried with the emperor when he died, to protect him in the afterlife.

LI SI was a powerful prime minister who helped the emperor unify and govern China.

XU FU was the official court sorcerer. He was employed to find a way of making the emperor live forever.

The emperor's son QIN ER SHI took over the empire after his father's death. He was not as capable as his father, so his reign was a time of great unrest.

The emperor was born Ying Zheng, but later gave himself the name QIN SHI HUANG, which means "First Emperor of China."

Legend has it that 3,000 CHILDREN were sent on an expedition to track down the wizard Anqi Sheng and find the secret of immortality.

Where next? From one amazing piece of architecture to another, we whizzed off to check out the Great Wall of China. This is where we found China's first emperor.

Qin Shi Huang was busy inspecting the wall, which was designed to keep invaders out of his enormous empire.

Now, this guy knew how to get things done. As well as being a ruthless warrior who unified China, he also standardized the Chinese language and currency, and even reduced congestion on the roads by insisting that all carts be the same width. He was a total control freak—he had millions of books burned so that he could write his own version of history!

He was also very superstitious: when a shooting star fell to earth, he heard it had an inscription saying that the emperor would die. Soon afterward, he did, apparently poisoned by pills that he thought would make him live forever!

AD 80, ITALY
GETTING READY FOR THE GLADIATORS

TITUS died of a fever after only two years as emperor at the age of 42.

The poet MARTIAL was very popular because of his witty, sometimes cheeky, poems about life in Rome.

In the crowd was a young boy named SUETONIUS, who would grow up to be a famous historian.

Gladiators rule, so I HAD to visit the Romans. But the Roman Empire lasted for so long, it was hard to decide which year to go!

After some help from the professor, I decided to go and see the building of the Colosseum in Rome, where the gladiators fought.
The Colosseum was... colossal! The prof told me that once the stadium was finished, it could seat up to 50,000 people who came to watch epic fights and chariot races. Sometimes they even flooded it to stage mock naval battles!

It was built on the orders of the Emperor Titus. As emperors go, it sounds like Titus was quite a decent guy. A successful military commander and a talented poet, he also did a lot to rebuild Rome after a massive fire. And a year before, when a volcano had erupted burying the towns of Pompeii and Herculaneum, he'd pulled out all the stops to help the people.

I started chatting with a gladiator and managed to hitch a ride around the stadium on a raging bull. When in Rome, eh?

Many CHILDREN were made homeless by a large fire in Rome, but the generosity of Titus meant they were quickly rehoused.

AD 970, CHINA
FIREWORKS FIT FOR A KING

EMPEROR TAIZU OF SONG
was the guest of honor. He had seized power illegally but reigned successfully for 16 years.

Fireworks are cool, so I jumped at the chance of seeing one of the world's first-ever displays. They were invented in China over 1,000 years ago.

They were made by packing chemicals and honey into bamboo sticks, which exploded when thrown on a fire. These sticks gave off a big bang, but weren't that impressive to look at. For a long time, they were just enjoyed by ordinary people and no one thought they were worth showing to the emperor. But as time passed, the fireworks grew larger and more spectacular, and when we arrived, a display was being put on for Emperor Taizu of Song.

If I'm honest, the display wasn't as amazing as others I've seen in modern times, but the fact that they'd worked out how to make fireworks at all 1,000 years ago is pretty impressive, isn't it? And when firecrackers were used in warfare—to scare soldiers and cause their horses to bolt—you can understand why people were terrified!

ZHAO GUANGYI treated his brother the emperor with respect, but was later accused of murdering him for the throne.

Accompanying the emperor was his third wife, **EMPRESS SONG**. When they got married, he was 40 but she was only 17!

PRINCE YI OF YAN was the emperor's son. Some people think that he was killed by his uncle after his father died.

The emperor's youngest son, **ZHAO DEFANG**, was only 11 years old. He was captivated by the fireworks!

► AD 1000, CANADA
SAILING TO THE NEW WORLD

One of the crewmen, a German named **TYRKER**, is thought to have found the vines after getting lost in the woods.

Leif's brother **THORVALD** was the first of the Vikings to spot the indigenous Americans already living there.

FREYDÍS EIRÍKSDÓTTIR, Leif's sister, was among those who traveled to Vinland, where the Vikings built a small settlement.

Accompanying Leif were his sons **THORGILS** and **THORKELL**, who returned to Greenland and eventually became important chieftains.

I know that humans are great explorers—venturing to the depths of the ocean and even into space. And so, I thought, how cool would it be to join one of humankind's early expeditions?

For centuries people believed Christopher Columbus was the first European to visit the Americas, but the professor told me that a Viking named Leif Erikson actually got there nearly 500 years earlier. Off we went to join him!

He moved with his family to Greenland after his father was exiled from Iceland for killing a man in a fight (glad we didn't have to meet HIM). Leif was a good sailor, and after hearing stories of a land many miles to the west, he decided to search for it. With a crew of 35, he set sail in a small open boat, and managed to make it across hundreds of miles of ocean. They arrived in what we now call Newfoundland, in Canada. They called it "Vinland" because there were loads of grapevines (handy, because I'd been feeling a bit queasy after the journey—a few refreshing grapes made me feel better). The coast there was rugged and desolate, and the landscape stretched for miles—I felt like I was on the edge of the world!

The Vikings called the local people "SKRÆLINGJAR," meaning "foreigners," although, of course, the sailors were the foreign ones!

1200, MEXICO
SPOTTING THE SUN SERPENT

An important building at Chichen Itza was a round **OBSERVATORY**. This had a window that showed the appearance of the planet Venus once every eight years.

Each face of the pyramid had a staircase with 91 steps. Together with the shared step at the top, these added up to **365**: the number of days in a year.

So what was going on elsewhere in the Americas? I'd heard about the amazing pyramid temple at Chichen Itza in Mexico, so why not pay a visit and meet the Mayans at the same time?

The Mayan people lived in Central America for a couple of thousand years. Apparently they were amazing at astronomy. They didn't have telescopes or any of that jazz—they just watched the skies carefully and made observations. They were able to trace the movements of the sun, stars, and planets, which they believed were gods.

The Mayans made super-smart calendars and could even predict when eclipses were going to happen. They based a lot of stuff around astronomy, planting their crops and waging wars to tie in with the movements of the stars.

We arrived in the town of Chichen Itza in the middle of some sort of ceremony. Loads of people were gathered around serpent pyramid, and all of a sudden one of the priests held up his arms and made an announcement. Everyone went quiet. As we watched, the sun fell across the pyramid, casting a strange shadow that made it look like a snake was slithering down from the top. Cooool!

The **STEP PYRAMID** at Chichen Itza was a temple dedicated to the serpent god Kukulcan.

1206, INDIA
FROM A SLAVE... TO A SULTAN!

The **QUTB MINAR** is 238 feet tall and was used to call people to prayer.

Aybak was determined to make his country a safer place—any **BANDITS** caught robbing travelers were quickly imprisoned.

QUTB-UD-DIN AYBAK was known for his great generosity.

The QUWWWAT-UL-ISLAM MOSQUE was built by Aybak and was the first mosque in Delhi.

TURKAN KHATUN was a former servant girl who married Iltutmish and became queen.

ILTUTMISH became sultan after Aybak died. His daughter RAZIYYA AL-DIN eventually became the first woman to rule over Delhi.

I love a rags-to-riches story, so when the prof told me that one of history's most powerful Indian rulers had once been a slave, I decided to see him for myself.

As a child, Qutb-ud-din Aybak was sold into slavery, but rose through the ranks by wowing his masters with his military skill. He was made a general and a governor before finally becoming the first sultan of Delhi. Impressive!

The professor said that as the first Muslim ruler in South Asia, the new sultan quickly set about modernizing his country and constructing great mosques. We saw a beautiful tower called the Qutb Minar being built.

Sadly, only four years after becoming sultan, Aybak died from falling off his horse while playing polo. One of his own slaves, named Iltutmish, came to the throne after his master's death. Rags to riches all over again!

Religion was very important to Genghis Khan. He frequently asked religious figures for advice, including a Taoist monk named **QIU CHUJI**.

Genghis Khan's son **CHAGATAI** was a bit of a hothead, but he grew up to be a good ruler.

GENGHIS KHAN had a difficult childhood. His father was poisoned by a rival tribe, and Genghis himself was captured and enslaved.

BÖRTE was the khan's wife and Grand Empress. Their ten children helped rule the huge empire.

The **REEVE** in Chaucer's tale was bad-tempered and dishonest. His job was to look after his master's lands.

Tall, brave, and handsome, the **KNIGHT** in *The Canterbury Tales* tells a story about two cousins in competition for the love of a beautiful lady.

One of Chaucer's most famous characters was the **WIFE OF BATH**. Larger than life, she had been married five times!

Time to chill! After hanging out with some pretty powerful people, I needed a bit of downtime with some normal folk.

The professor suggested a trip to medieval London, and we arrived outside a busy tavern on the bank of the River Thames.

The air was full of sounds and smells—traders shouting, horses whinnying, the stink of manure, stale beer, and roasting meat. In the bustle we spotted Geoffrey Chaucer, who was one of the great poets of the Middle Ages, so the prof says.

Chaucer's most famous book is called *The Canterbury Tales*, and it's about a group of travelers on a pilgrimage to a shrine in Canterbury. A pilgrimage was a journey to a holy place, and in those days, it was often the only chance people got to travel, so going on a pilgrimage was a bit like going on vacation... only without a car or plane to get there! In Chaucer's book, the pilgrims entertained each other on the long journey by telling stories, which were often funny and quite rude.

At the beginning of a pilgrimage, travelers would often meet up at a tavern. Outside this tavern were a load of colorful characters—I bet the pilgrims in Chaucer's stories were based on real people!

1439, GERMANY
GUTENBERG, HOT OFF THE PRESS!

Sadly, **GUTENBERG** failed to make his fortune from printing, but after he died, the popularity of his invention spread quickly.

Stop the presses! Owning a printer today may be no big deal, but it turns out the invention of the printing press way back in the 15th century was a bit of a game changer.

Before printing, books had to be copied out by hand, which took, well... a long time. The inventor of the press was a hard-working blacksmith named Johannes Gutenberg, and when we popped in, we found his workshop in Mainz buzzing with activity.

The press was a gigantic wooden contraption with loads of little wooden letter blocks. Gutenberg arranged the letters on the machine to make pages of writing, then rolled them in ink and pressed them onto paper. He was rushing around so fast, I thought he might trap his long beard in the mechanism!

The professor reckons that we saw Gutenberg working on the worlds first printed Bible. A few copies have survived, and are among the most valuable books in the world today. Anyway, the press was such an important invention because it meant that books could be made quickly and cheaply, spreading knowledge to millions of people. Go, Gutenberg!

ENNELIN ZU DER ISERIN TUR, whose name means "Anne of the Iron Door," hoped to marry Gutenberg, but the wedding never took place.

1492, THE BAHAMAS
REDISCOVERING THE NEW WORLD!

RODRIGO BERNAJO spotted the island, shouting "Tierra!" (which means "land"). Later, Columbus claimed that he had seen it first.

The **LUCAYANS** were the indigenous people of the Bahamas. The explorers called them "Indians" because they mistakenly thought they were in the Indies.

Something was confusing me. I'd just seen Leif Erikson landing in Canada, so why did everyone say that Christopher Columbus discovered the Americas?

The professor knows a thing or two about this guy. Christopher Columbus was an Italian explorer who'd been sent by the king and queen of Spain to find a new route from Europe to the Far East: India, China, and Japan. He knew that the world was round, and believed that if he headed west, he would eventually reach China. Turns out he got a bit lost, and ended up in the Bahamas instead.

This was a Big Deal because it changed the course of history, opening up the world for the explorers and traders that followed. But Columbus didn't "discover" the Americas, because there were people living there already! Plus, Leif Erikson had gotten there 500 years before, but his voyage was a bit of a one-off that was forgotten by history. Although Columbus later visited South America, he never actually set foot in North America.

Anyway, we were lucky enough to join him at the end of his ten-week-long voyage, just as his crew of three ships and 90 men reached an island that he later named San Salvador. We noticed that a guy named Rodrigo Bernajo was actually the first sailor to sight land, but Columbus took the credit for himself!

After his voyage, **COLUMBUS** was appointed governor of the Indies. He was a very brutal, unpopular ruler.

PEDRO DE TERREROS was the cabin boy on the *Santa María*, the largest of Columbus's ships.

At first, Columbus struggled to win the aid of **QUEEN ISABELLA** and **KING FERDINAND**, but eventually the Spanish monarchs gave their support.

For centuries, no one was sure who the lady in the painting was, but most people now believe her to be **LISA DEL GIOCONDO**, the wife of an Italian merchant.

FRANCESCO DEL GIOCONDO was a wealthy merchant who asked Da Vinci to paint his wife.

NICCOLÒ MACHIAVELLI was a writer and politician. He wrote a book, *The Prince*, about power and politics, where he advised rulers to be ruthless.

I'd always wanted to see the world's most famous painting, the *Mona Lisa*, so what could be better than watching it actually being made?

The guy who painted it, Leonardo da Vinci, was a bit of a genius. Not only was he an amazing painter and sculptor, but he was also an architect, engineer, mathematician, and inventor. One of his sketchbooks includes a design for a helicopter, drawn hundreds of years before anyone managed to fly. He even devised a secret way of writing to stop people finding out what he was up to.

The *Mona Lisa* is a portrait of a mysterious lady. It took years to finish, but not because it was large or complicated. The problem was that Da Vinci was always getting distracted by other projects. While we were watching him, he kept racing off and scribbling things down in his notebooks. Poor old Mona Lisa looked a bit annoyed!

While we were in Florence we also tracked down the artist Michelangelo, and I even managed to help out a bit with a new statue he was making. It looked pretty cool. I'd hoped that while we were there I might get to try some gelato (Italian ice cream) but annoyingly we were just a few years too early and it hadn't been invented yet. Oh well.

▶ 1599, BRITAIN
SHAKESPEARE TREADS THE BOARDS

Theater performances were accompanied by live music from the **MINSTRELS' GALLERY**.

RICHARD BURBAGE was a famous actor and one of the owners of the Globe Theatre. He played lots of main roles, such as Hamlet and King Lear.

SHAKESPEARE was an actor as well as being the most popular playwright of his time.

Once I'd had my fix of painting and sculpture, I was craving a trip to the theater, so off we headed to the Globe in London, where they were putting on the latest play by William Shakespeare.

These days, a theater visit can be quite a fancy affair where you have to be on your best behavior, but not back then! For starters, the wooden building was open to the sky... lucky for us it wasn't raining that day!

Richer members of the audience sat in the gallery, but others (called groundlings) stood in the yard, eating, drinking, talking, jeering, and laughing rudely, sometimes throwing moldy apples at the performers if they weren't enjoying the play.

Striding onto the straw-covered stage, Shakespeare looked exactly as I'd imagined him. The professor blushed, totally star-struck. (She's a massive fan.) "That's him!" she hissed. "The world's greatest playwright, right in front of us!"

We looked around to see who else we could spot, and the prof pointed out Sir Walter Raleigh, Dr. John Dee, and even Queen Elizabeth I in the audience. What luck!

QUEEN ELIZABETH I reigned for nearly half a century. During this time, England became richer and more powerful than ever before.

The great explorer SIR WALTER RALEIGH returned from his travels across the world with exotic souvenirs. Legend has it that he introduced the potato to Britain.

DR. JOHN DEE was the queen's most trusted scientific adviser. He fascinated her with his knowledge of mathematics, magic, and the stars.

Shakespeare dedicated two of his poems to a young nobleman named Henry Wriothesley, EARL OF SOUTHAMPTON.

1682, FRANCE
A ROYAL WELCOME IN VERSAILLES

The king's favorite landscape designer was **ANDRÉ LE NÔTRE**. At Versailles, he created the greatest gardens in Europe, which covered more than three square miles.

Louis and his Spanish queen, **MARIA THERESA**, had six children, but five of them died in childhood.

1761, AUSTRIA
MAKING MUSIC WITH MOZART

The **DUKE OF BAVARIA** loved music and enjoyed Mozart's playing. Through him, the child was invited to perform in many royal palaces.

The **ARCHBISHOP OF SALZBURG** employed Mozart's father as a violinist. He was the first of many influential people to hear the young Mozart play.

MOZART lived to be only 35. During his short life, he wrote more music than many composers twice his age. In total, he composed more than 600 pieces, including operas and symphonies.

I didn't want to miss the chance to meet one of the world's most gifted child prodigies, Wolfgang Amadeus Mozart.

Mozart's music career began when he was only three. After watching his sister playing an instrument called the clavinet, he decided to try it himself. Copying her finger movements, he found the keyboard surprisingly easy to play, and was soon getting to grips with more advanced pieces.

By the time he was five, he was composing music of his own. And thanks to my yellow pencil, I was able to witness his amazing talents firsthand! News of his extraordinary abilities quickly spread throughout Europe, and within a year, the boy was performing for royalty at the court of Empress Maria Theresa of Austria.

Mozart seemed like a happy, fun-loving little guy, and I could see that his success was well-deserved. He was awesome!

Known as **NANNERL**, Mozart's sister Maria was a talented musician whose concerts often included pieces written by her younger brother.

Mozart's father, **LEOPOLD**, was also his music teacher. Leopold took his clever children to play concerts all over Europe.

When he was 14, Mozart heard a beautiful choral piece called the "**MISERERE**" performed in Rome. He was so enchanted by the music that he managed to write out the entire score from memory!

▶ 1805, USA
CROSSING AMERICA WITH LEWIS AND CLARK

LIEUTENANT CLARK had been in the army and used his skills to hunt for food. He also took care of creating maps on the expedition.

SACAGAWEA was a Shoshone woman who accompanied the expedition, acting as an interpreter. She gave birth to a baby, Jean Baptiste, in February 1805.

In 1803, the third president of the United States, Thomas Jefferson, sent Captain Meriwether Lewis and William Clark to explore the western part of North America.

They aimed to map the previously uncharted area, find a route to the Pacific Ocean, learn as much as they could about the area's Native American peoples, and study the plants and animals. A pretty wide brief! The grueling expedition took several years—after two bitter winters and many thousands of miles of traveling, they finally made it to the Pacific Ocean in November 1805.

We joined them as they traveled down the Columbia River. It was a bit of a tight squeeze in the canoe, especially as I was crammed in next to a massive dog. Random! There was a harsh wind across the water—I wished I was wearing some of the warm-looking clothes that the others had on. Suddenly, a shout went up from Lieutenant Clark—"Ocean in view!" Everyone looked pretty happy about that.

Before he set out, **CAPTAIN LEWIS** took a crash course both in medicine and navigation.

Ada's mentor and tutor, **MARY SOMERVILLE**, was the joint first female member of the Royal Astronomical Society. She introduced Ada to Babbage.

One of Ada's friends, the mathematician **LUIGI MENABREA**, later became prime minister of Italy.

In 1835, Ada Byron married **WILLIAM KING**. He was made Earl of Lovelace soon after, so Ada became Countess of Lovelace.

CHARLES BABBAGE'S mathematical and mechanical skill could be seen from a young age. As a child, he would take toys apart to see how they worked.

Ada's mother separated from her father, **LORD BYRON**, when Ada was only a few weeks old. Her mother encouraged Ada to study sciences, hoping that this would stop her from becoming moody and unpredictable like her father!

When **ADA LOVELACE** died, she owed thousands of pounds in gambling debts after disastrously trying to use her maths skills to win on the horses.

When scientists were nearly all men, and women from upper-class families rarely worked, Ada Lovelace must have been pretty extraordinary. She was the daughter of the poet Lord Byron and was a super-smart mathematician.

When I found her, she was deep in conversation with a guy named Charles Babbage. He had built the world's first computer. It was massive and looked totally complicated—not much like my laptop back home. He called it his Analytical Engine.

The professor says that Ada was fascinated by it and hooked on the idea of using it to solve difficult mathematical problems. She wrote up some notes on the machine, and in these notes was the world's first "algorithm": a set of instructions needed to complete a calculation.

Today, computer coders use algorithms all the time, and Ada Lovelace has gone down in history as the world's first programmer. Not bad for the daughter of a crazy poet!

The politician **THADDEUS STEVENS** was a fierce opponent of slavery and was crucially important in getting the Thirteenth Amendment passed.

After escaping from slavery, **FREDERICK DOUGLASS** became a leader of the antislavery movement. He was an amazing public speaker.

ULYSSES S. GRANT was a general who led the northern armies to victory in the Civil War. He later became president.

SOJOURNER TRUTH was born into slavery but escaped with her baby daughter in 1826. She became one of America's most persuasive antislavery campaigners.

Just five days after the end of the Civil War, **PRESIDENT LINCOLN** was shot while at the theater in Washington, D.C. He died the next morning.

HARRIET BEECHER STOWE wrote a book called *Uncle Tom's Cabin*, a story about life for African American slaves. It was read by millions, and helped turn people against slavery.

With not many pages left in my notebook, I couldn't miss the chance of meeting the famous American president Abraham Lincoln, so off we whizzed to Washington.

We found ourselves in the middle of a huge crowd on a cold January day. Ahead of us was the Capitol building, grand against the blue sky. People all around were cheering and hugging, waving flags and throwing their hats in the air. Over the noise, the professor managed to explain the reason for the celebrations: slavery in America had just been made illegal. The Thirteenth Amendment to the Constitution, abolishing slavery, had been voted into law.

Slavery had been a part of life here for over 200 years. By 1820, the Northern states were mostly against it, while the Southern states wanted it to continue because their economy needed slave labor. This disagreement became a key part of the American Civil War, where the Northern states went to war against the Southern states. The president, Abraham Lincoln, led the Northern states to victory.

From here, we had a good view of the White House, where President Lincoln was waiting for news of the vote. The atmosphere was electric! It was chilling to think that only four months later, Lincoln would be assassinated.

Workers on the railway included **PRISONERS** and **SOLDIERS**. They had to live in incredibly cold, harsh conditions.

NICHOLAS II was first cousin to King George V of England and second cousin to Kaiser Wilhelm II of Germany.

The emperor's wife, **ALEXANDRA FEODOROVNA**, was one of Queen Victoria's granddaughters. She only rarely joined her husband on his travels.

The construction of the **TRANS-SIBERIAN RAILROAD** was the largest and most ambitious project of its kind ever undertaken.

PRINCE MIKHAIL KHILKOV, minister of transport, oversaw the building of the railway. He employed a workforce of more than 90,000 men to lay rails and signals across the vast frozen wastes of Siberia.

STEPAN MAKAROV designed the ice-breaker ferry SS *Baikal*. It was built in Britain, then immediately dismantled and sent to Russia. The parts were then put back together again on the lake.

OK, I admit it... I'm a bit of a trainspotter, so I couldn't resist a trip to check out the Trans-Siberian Railroad. After more than 100 years, it's still the longest railway on Earth, linking one side of the world's largest country with the other.

Starting from Russia's capital, Moscow, and finishing at the port of Vladivostok on the Sea of Japan, it's almost 6,000 miles long. Traveling from end to end takes nearly a week!

The professor filled me in on the history of the railway. It was the dream of Russia's last emperor, Nicholas II. He wanted to improve transport links between Russia and China to make trade easier.

One problem that the engineers had to contend with was Lake Baikal: the oldest and deepest lake on earth, lying right across the route of the railway. Tricky. Nowadays there's a track running around the southern shore, but back then the entire train had to be loaded onto a special ice-breaker ferry and shipped from one side of the lake to the other. Luckily, we arrived in the remote town of Lystvyanka just in time to see Nicholas himself paying a visit to inspect the boat. Brrrrr! It was nippy!

HENRI BECQUEREL was a French physicist who made some important discoveries about radioactivity. He shared the Nobel Prize with the Curies.

When Marie married the physicist **PIERRE CURIE**, he abandoned his own work to help with her research.

In 1934, **MARIE CURIE** died from leukemia caused by years of exposure to radiation in the course of her work.

Coming from a proudly academic family, Marie's sister **BRONISŁAWA DŁUSKA** qualified as a doctor of medicine and supported Marie financially.

The scientist Marie Curie was the first woman to win a Nobel Prize, so I was happy to be able to see her at work in her lab in Paris.

Born in Poland as Maria Skłodowska, she went to college in Paris and stayed there after she married a fellow scientist, Pierre Curie. They worked together, often late into the night, making important discoveries in the field of radioactivity. In 1903, they won the Nobel Prize for Physics, but they were too busy to go to Sweden to collect it!

This woman was a total groundbreaker. Not being content with one Nobel Prize, she won another eight years later, this time for Chemistry, and was also the first woman professor at the University of Paris. She discovered the chemical elements polonium (which she named after her home country) and radium, and her work led to the use of X-rays in medicine.

I found her laboratory surprisingly basic for a Nobel Prize winner: it was actually just a converted shed! The professor tells me that Curie couldn't afford a proper lab until later, in 1906. Anyway, we didn't hang around for long because we knew that soaking up too much radiation could be dangerous... Time to skedaddle!

Awarding the Nobel Prize to a woman was considered controversial at the time, but the Swedish mathematician **MAGNUS MITTAG-LEFFLER** insisted that Marie be honored as well as Pierre.

Marie Curie's tutor at college in Paris was **PROFESSOR GABRIEL LIPPMANN**, one of the inventors of color photography.

VOTES FOR WOMEN

Emmeline's daughters **CHRISTABEL** and **SYLVIA** were imprisoned many times because of their roles in the suffragette movement.

EMMELINE PANKHURST died only a few weeks after women were awarded equal voting rights to men in 1928.

I was amazed when the professor told me that only 100 years ago most women around the world weren't allowed to vote in elections. Nuts, eh?

In Britain, Emmeline Pankhurst wanted to change all this. She created the Women's Social and Political Union, who were known as the suffragettes. They held protests against the government, who were determined not to give them the vote. They broke up political meetings, chained themselves to railings, smashed windows, and even set politicians' houses on fire to make themselves heard. Suffragettes were often arrested and sent to prison, where they would go on hunger strike, refusing to eat until they were released.

At last, in 1918, women over 30 were given the vote in Britain, and ten years later they had the same rights to vote as men. On the other side of the Atlantic, a similar campaign fought by American women triumphed in 1920, when the Nineteenth Amendment gave them the vote. In Europe the suffrage movement had lots of victories, too.

We joined the suffragettes in the middle of a protest march. With banners flying, a brass band playing and voices chanting "Votes for Women!" it was easy to get caught up in the excitement. The professor pointed out Emmeline Pankhurst in the middle of the action. She looked like she meant business.

1935, AUSTRALIA
FLYING WITH NANCY-BIRD WALTON

These days, flying in a plane is a fairly safe way to get around. But back in the 1930s, it was a much more dangerous business.

There was less training for pilots and they had no detailed maps, no radios, no brakes, and few real runways. To stop a plane, the pilot had to turn off the engine, then glide back to earth in a series of turns. Scary stuff!

One of the earliest Australian pilots was Nancy-Bird Walton. At only 19, she became Australia's youngest licensed female pilot—pretty impressive when you consider that at the time most people thought a woman's place was in the home.

We dropped in on her as she was soaring over the Australian outback. Apparently, she was a bit of a lifesaver. Literally. She was the first person to fly an air ambulance for Far West Children's Health Scheme. She flew out to remote farms, carrying nurses to help families who needed medical care, or transporting sick people to the hospital. It was a tough job, if you ask me. It was so hot—it must have been about 100 degrees. Imagine being crammed into a noisy, tiny cockpit all day in the sweltering heat, not knowing whether you were going to land safely! What a hero.

NANCY-BIRD WALTON set up the Australian Women Pilots' Association in 1950 and was awarded an OBE by the Queen in 1966.

Many **AUSTRALIAN FARMS** were hundreds of miles away from the nearest town, making it impossible to get to the hospital in a hurry.

Nancy left school at age 13 so she could help her **FATHER** run his business. Later, her dad loaned her the money to buy her first plane.

REVEREND STANLEY DRUMMOND set up the Far West Children's Health Scheme and got Nancy-Bird involved. It's still going strong today.

The Jamaican political leader **MARCUS GARVEY** became an important civil rights activist.

LANGSTON HUGHES was a poet, novelist, and playwright.

EDWARD HOPPER was a famous American painter.

When you think of a genius, you think of Einstein, right? I had to see the great man for myself, so I paid a visit to the Big Apple in the 1930s.

Professor Tempo told me that Albert Einstein fled Germany after the Nazis came to power in 1933. Like many Jews, his life was in danger. He escaped to New York, where they were pleased as punch to have him. Einstein was a brilliant professor who had already won the Nobel Prize in Physics as well as heaps more international awards.

One of America's top universities offered him a new home right away. They recognized that his research was vital in improving our understanding of how the universe works. I'm no Einstein, so his complicated theories were a bit over my head, but he seemed like a friendly dude and he took a break from his studies to show me around.

The prof had mentioned that Einstein believed time travel was impossible, so I didn't let on that I was from the future—it wouldn't have been cool to give the guy a heart attack!

"BABE" RUTH played baseball for the New York Yankees. He set many sports records that no one managed to break for years.

A popular antiwar campaigner, **JEANNETTE RANKIN** was the first woman elected to the United States Congress.

1964, JAPAN
CATCHING A BULLET IN TOKYO!

SHINJI SOGŌ, the president of Japanese National Railways, arranged for the first train to run between Osaka and Tokyo in time for the 1964 Olympic Games.

The Ethiopian athlete ABEBE BIKILA became the first person ever to win two Olympic marathons. He had also won the 1960 marathon in Rome, where he competed barefoot.

The American boxer **"SMOKIN'" JOE FRAZIER** won a gold medal at the Tokyo Olympics. He went on to become Heavyweight World Champion in 1970.

Japan's prime minister, **KAKUEI TANAKA**, was a great supporter of railways. He could see the benefits of a high-speed train service.

YOSHINORI SAKAI was born in Hiroshima in 1945 on the same day the city was destroyed by an atomic bomb. He had the honor of lighting the Olympic Flame.

Next stop, and we were off to Tokyo to combine two of my big loves: sports and trains.

For years, the bullet trains on Japan's high-speed rail network were the fastest and most advanced in the world. And the first bullet train opened just a few days before the 1964 Olympics in Tokyo. What a rush to be able to travel on one myself!

With most of Japan's population spread over four large islands, millions of people regularly travel massive distances to get to work. The high-speed railway was the brainchild of Hideo Shima, an engineer who set out to design trains that were not only fast but also comfortable and super safe. They built thousands of new bridges and tunnels between Japan's major cities so that the new trains could run in straight lines over long distances. The first train traveled at over 125 miles per hour, which was handy because it meant we were on time to watch the Olympics. These Olympic Games were much more familiar to me than the ancient Greek ones. For a start, everyone had clothes on this time!

► 1969, THE MOON
MANKIND'S GIANT LEAP...

The **MOON'S CLIMATE** is extremely harsh. In the sun's glare the temperature can reach a scorching 250°F, but in the shadows it falls to a blisteringly cold -240°F!

NO ONE has been to the moon for more than 40 years, but people still hope to build a colony there one day.

Well, it's been a pretty amazing journey. I've visited some incredible places and met some of the most awesome folks ever to have lived on earth. So, where do you think I picked for my last stop? Where else? The moon!

In 1903, the world's first manned airplane managed to fly just over 120 feet before bumping back down to earth. After that, it took just 66 years for humans to make a rocket to fly to the moon, and—thanks to my magic pencil—we were there to see it touch down.

How mind-blowing to think that the astronauts' journey took them about 40 million times farther than the Wright brothers' first flight! Impressive that such progress could have been made in less than one single lifetime.

Neil Armstrong famously described his first small step on the moon as a giant leap for mankind, and over the next three years, just 11 other people were lucky enough to follow him. Now the race is on to be the first person to visit Mars. I can't wait to find out who it will be! Hmm, I wonder if my yellow pencil could take me to the future...?

Two astronauts walked on the moon that famous day in 1969. **NEIL ARMSTRONG** stepped out of the Lunar Module first, and Buzz Aldrin followed soon after. Their colleague Michael Collins stayed on board the orbiting spacecraft.

THE SUITS worn by the astronauts cost an estimated $100,000 each! They were vital to protect them from the intense temperatures on the moon.

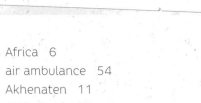
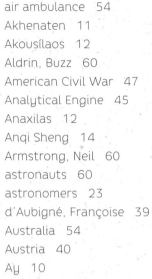

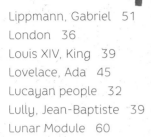

Wide Eyed Editions
www.wideeyededitions.com

First published in the United States in 2015 by Wide Eyed Editions
an imprint of Quarto Inc.,
276 Fifth Avenue, Suite 206, New York, NY 10001.
www.wideeyededitions.com

ISBN 978-1-84780-704-5

The illustrations were created digitally
Set in Fugue, Core Rhino, and Lunch Box

Designed by Nicola Price
Edited by Emily Hawkins and Jenny Broom
Published by Rachel Williams

Printed in Shenzhen, Guangdong, China

1 3 5 7 9 8 6 4 2

TO FIND OUT MORE...
CHECK OUT THESE GREAT RESOURCES

A REALLY SHORT HISTORY OF NEARLY EVERYTHING
by Bill Bryson
This book explores the history of science,
right back to the beginning of time.
Delacorte Books for Young Readers 2009

BBC HISTORY
Enter ancient worlds, meet famous
people, and discover fascinating facts
with this online resource
http://www.bbc.co.uk/history/forkids/

THE BRITISH MUSEUM
Explore this vast archive, which is
themed by culture, by place, by people,
by material, and by popularity!
http://www.britishmuseum.org/explore

HISTORY FOR KIDS
A kid's-eye-view on everything from
Ancient Greece and Rome through to
America history.
http://www.historyforkids.net/

KIDS PAST
A compendium of world history
provided by the Totally Free Children's
Learning Network
http://www.kidspast.com/